Living Nature

FLOWERS

Chrysalis Children's Books

The publishers wish to thank the following for permission to reproduce copyright material:

Oxford Scientific Films and individual copyright holders on the following pages: George I Bernard 17 top, 20 left; Deni Brown 14 bottom, 24 top; Arthur Butler 4 top right; David Cayless 11 centre right; John Chellman/Earth Scenes 4 bottom left; Densey Clyne 21 bottom; J A L Cooke 16 bottom right; L M Crowhurst 20 right; David Curl 27; John Gerlach/ Earth Scenes 6 bottom; Mark Hamblin 7 bottom right, 24 bottom; Christian B. Hvidt/Foci 14 top; Breck P Kent/Animals Animals 15 bottom, 24 centre; Geoff Kidd 12 top; London Scientific Films 26 top; G A MacLeann 5 top right, 12 bottom; B G Murray Jr title page; Stan Osolinski 13, 17 bottom; Oxford Scientific Films 11 top right, 18 right; Richard Packwood 5 bottom, 7 top; Peter Parks 6 top right; Partridge Productions Ltd 19; Avril Ramage 28/29; Hans Reinhard/Okapia 26 bottom; Kjell Sandved 15 top; Perry D Slocum/Earth Scenes, contents page; Harold Taylor 11 bottom, 25.

This edition first published in 2003 by

Chrysalis Children's Books
The Chrysalis Building, Bramley Rd,
London W10 6SP

Text copyright © Angela Royston
Photographs copyright © Oxford Scientific Films and individual copyright holders
Format and illustrations © Chrysalis Books PLC

Printed in Hong Kong

ISBN 1 84138 633 2

British Library Cataloguing in Publication Data CIP data for this book is available from the British Library

A Belitha Book

Editor: Serpentine Editorial
Series designer: Frances McKay
Consultant: Andrew Branson

Text words in **bold** are in the glossary on page 30.

Title page:
Honeysuckle flowers have a strong scent.

Contents page:
A Carolina lily.

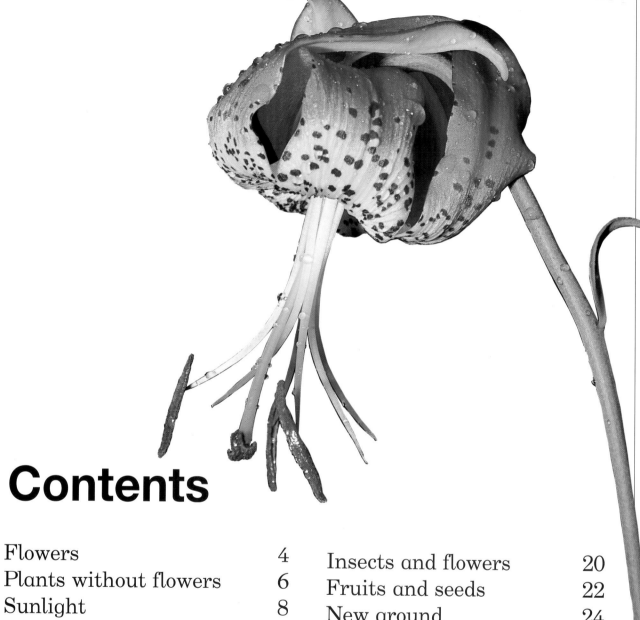

Contents

Flowers

Sometimes the word flower
can mean a whole plant,
like a cowslip. But a cowslip
has leaves, stems and roots,
as well as flowers.

▲ Cowslips
grow in grassy
places, beside the
road and in meadows.
They flower in early spring
and have a sweet smell.

◀ Orchids vary in
shape and size,
and some have
spectacular flowers.
Many orchids grow
in rainforests.

▶ Trees have
flowers, too.
In early spring the horse
chestnut has tall, white flowers.

It grows in the soil. A flower is only part of a plant. There are many kinds of flowering plants. They include trees, shrubs and plants such as orchids, which grow on trees, not in the soil.

▲ Sweet briar is a kind of wild rose. It has thorny stems and five heart-shaped petals.

Plants without flowers

▲ Euglena are tiny plants that swim around in water. You need a microscope to see them.

◄ The giant sequoia is the world's biggest tree. Its seeds grow in cones, not in flowers.

New plants grow from seeds. Most plants make seeds in their flowers. But the plants shown here do not have flowers. These plants make their seeds in other ways.

▲ Mosses and ferns grow well in damp places. Instead of flowers, they have millions of tiny **spores** which grow into new plants.

▶ The tip of a new fern is coiled. As the fern grows, the tip slowly uncurls upwards.

Did you know?

Ferns, mosses and trees with cones were growing 300 million years ago. Flowering plants did not start to grow until 100 million years ago.

Sunlight

Animals and plants need food to stay alive. Plants make their own food. Animals either eat plants or hunt other animals. Plants use sunlight to help to produce food. This process is called **photosynthesis**. Most of the food is made in the plant's leaves. They contain a green substance called **chlorophyll**.

▶ Plants use sunlight, carbon dioxide from the air and water from the soil to make sugar. Only the green parts of a plant can make food.

water   water

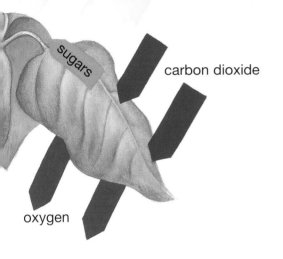

sunlight

sugars

carbon dioxide

oxygen

Chlorophyll takes in some of the energy in sunlight. The plant uses the energy to make sugar from the gas **carbon dioxide** and water. It turns sugar into starch. As well as making sugar, photosynthesis produces the gas **oxygen**. Plants and animals need to breathe in oxygen to stay alive. Without plants nothing could live on Earth.

◀ A hawk hunts a blue tit, which eats caterpillars, which feed on leaves. All animals rely on plants for food. When plants and animals die, the bodies rot and make the soil rich so that more plants can grow.

Roots

Roots have two main jobs —
they keep the plant upright
in the ground and they take
in water and minerals to help
it grow. The roots of this oak
tree reach as wide under the
ground as the branches
spread into the air. The
roots spread out as the
plant grows.

Did you know?

Some plants grow 100 million
new root hairs every day. As the
roots push through the soil, their
fine root hairs are rubbed off.

▶ Behind the
tip of each root
are millions of
fine hairs. The
hairs take in
water from
the soil.

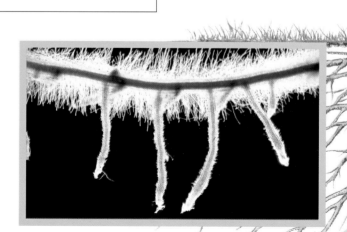

oak tree

▶ A carrot has a large tap root. It is a store of food for the plant and for us.

▲ Marram grass grows on sand dunes. It has long roots which spread out in all directions. The roots hold the sand dune together.

Just behind the root tips are very fine hairs which take in water from the soil. Some plants, such as carrots and beetroots, have one main root called a tap root.

Stems

Stems hold the different parts of a plant together. They carry water from the roots and food from the leaves to all other parts of the plant.

New leaves, shoots, and sometimes flowers, grow from the stems. They grow first as buds. Some stems grow under the ground and some are protected by spines and thorns.

▲ A tree trunk is a very big stem. The ivy winding around it has a much thinner, bendy stem.

Did you know?

A potato is a swollen underground stem called a tuber. It stores food for the plant. The eyes of a potato are the buds of new leaves.

▼ The stem of this rose is covered with spiky thorns. Thorns protect the plant from large animals that might want to eat it.

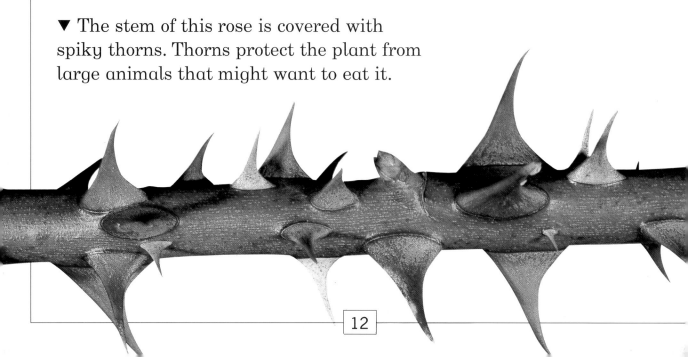

◄ A cactus stem
is full of water.
It is protected by
rows of spines.

Leaves

Some leaves have simple shapes – round, oval, heart-shaped, or long and thin. Other leaves have more complicated shapes.

◀ Many plants have simple-shaped leaves like this one. All leaves are criss-crossed with tiny veins.

▼ Holly has glossy, spiky leaves. The gloss keeps the leaves watertight and the spikes stop animals eating them.

Most of the plant's food is made in the leaves (see pages 8 and 9). The leaves turn towards the light. Small **veins** in each leaf carry water from the stem. Tiny holes in the leaves open to let the plant breathe in air.

▲ The curly thread is the tendril of a creeping vine. It helps the vine hold on to nearby plants.

▼ The leaves of some plants grow from a single bud but split into many smaller leaflets. They have a central leaf stalk.

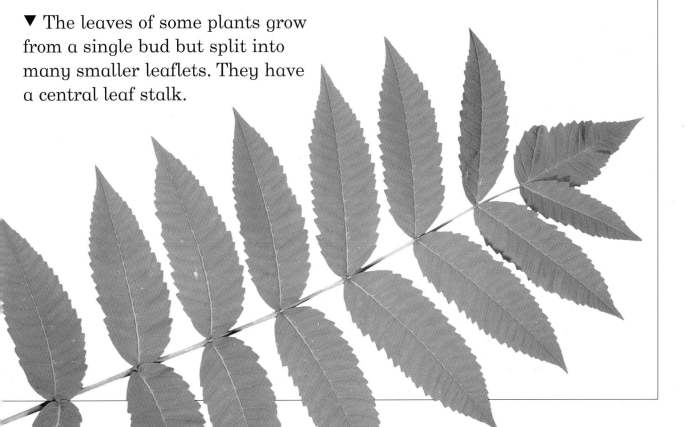

Petals

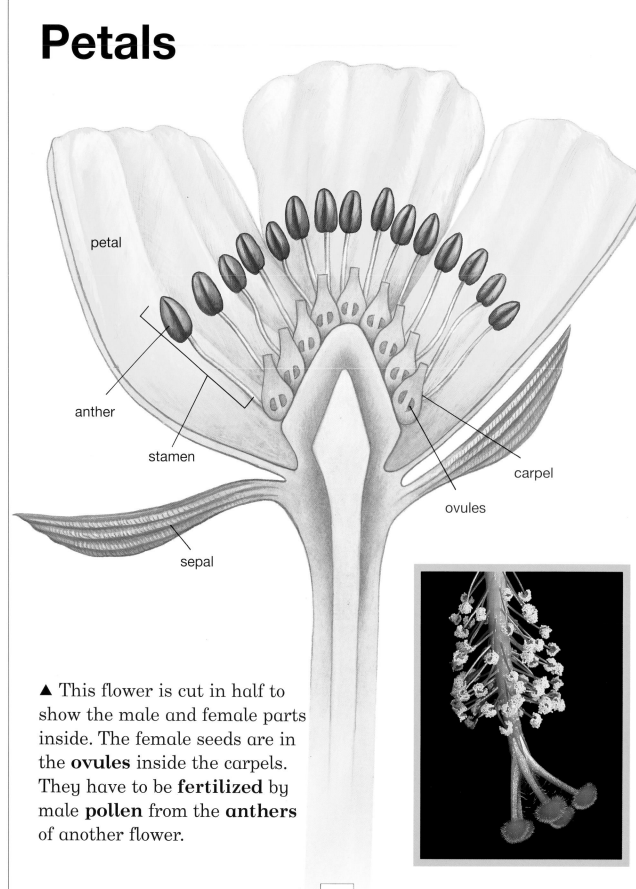

petal

anther

stamen

sepal

carpel

ovules

▲ This flower is cut in half to show the male and female parts inside. The female seeds are in the **ovules** inside the carpels. They have to be **fertilized** by male **pollen** from the **anthers** of another flower.

Flowers vary in colour, shape and size, but they are made up of the same parts. Most flowers have brightly-coloured petals. Outside the petals are green sepals. They covered and protected the flower when it was a bud. Inside the petals are **stamens** and **carpels**. These are the male and female parts of the flower.

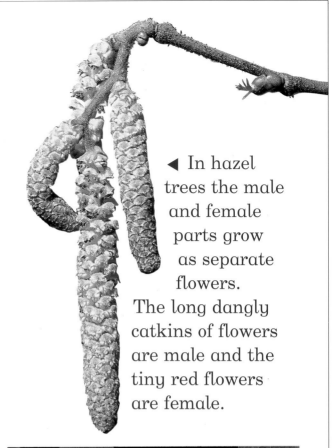

◄ In hazel trees the male and female parts grow as separate flowers. The long dangly catkins of flowers are male and the tiny red flowers are female.

◄ The male and female parts of a hibiscus flower. Yellow pollen clings to the male stamens. Below them are the pink female carpels.

► A daisy is not just one flower but several tiny yellow flowers packed together. The tiny flowers are surrounded by white petals.

Pollen

The job of a flower is to produce seeds to grow into new plants. To do this the female seeds must each join with a grain of male pollen from another flower. Pollen lands on the sticky top of the carpel.

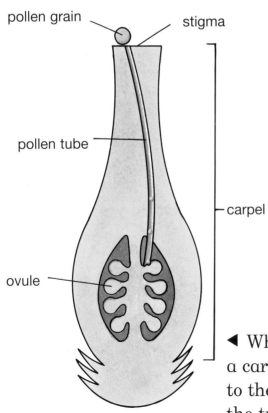

▲ Rye grass has tiny flowers packed together on the stems. When the wind blows the grass, fine clouds of pollen dust rise into the air.

◄ When a grain of pollen lands on a carpel, it grows a fine tube down to the ovule. The pollen passes down the tube and joins with one of the seeds. The seed is then fertilized.

▲ Some
animals help
to pollinate flowers.
As this fruit bat licks
sugary nectar inside the flower,
some of the pollen rubs off on
to its nose and mouth.

The process of getting the pollen to the female seeds is called pollination. Some pollen is spread by the wind. But most pollen is carried by insects, which take it from one flower to another (see pages 20 and 21).

Did you know?

Pollen is so light it sometimes travels hundreds of kilometres. The pollen of oak, pine and birch trees has been found in the middle of the Atlantic Ocean.

Insects and flowers

Many insects, including bees, moths, beetles and flies, pollinate flowers. But they do not know that they are carrying pollen from one flower to another.

Insects visit flowers to look for food – a sweet liquid called nectar. Bees make honey from the nectar and some kinds of beetles eat the pollen itself.

▶ Many plants produce a sugary liquid called nectar. This moth is using its long tongue to reach the nectar in the flowers.

◀ As the bee moves from flower to flower, its body becomes covered with pollen.

Flowers attract insects in several ways. Insects see more colours than we do and have a very good sense of smell. Flowers that are pollinated by insects usually have brightly-coloured petals and a sweet smell.

nectary

stamens

▲ This flower has been cut in half to show what happens when a bee visits a flower. As the bee reaches for the nectar, it touches the stamens and grains of pollen stick to its body.

▶ Rafflesias grow in south-east Asia. They are the world's biggest flower and have the worst smell. Insects love the smell of rotting meat.

Fruits and seeds

When a flower's seeds have been fertilized, the petals dry up and fall off. The carpels begin to swell and form fruits around the seeds to protect them. Inside each seed is a tiny new plant and a store of food to feed the plant until it has grown leaves and can make its own food.

▲ Inside each broad bean is a tiny plant.

◀ Broad beans form inside a pod.

▲The hard stone in the middle of each of these juicy cherries is a single seed.

Did you know?

The coco de mer palm has the world's biggest seeds – each nut weighs up to 18 kilograms. They grow on the Seychelles islands.

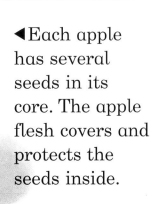

◀Each apple has several seeds in its core. The apple flesh covers and protects the seeds inside.

▶ The star fruit is named after its shape. Its seeds are in the centre.

Cucumbers, tomatoes, beans, and many things we call vegetables, are really fruits with seeds. Nuts are fruits, too. They grow inside hard shells. Many fruits are sweet and juicy. When they are ripe, animals eat them and scatter the seeds.

▼ The tiny pips on the outside of strawberries are the seeds.

▶ A blackberry is a cluster of tiny fruits. Each fruitlet has a seed in the middle.

▼ We think of cucumber as a vegetable, but it is really a fruit. The seeds run right down the middle.

▼ Horse chestnuts, or conkers, are fruits with seeds, too. They are protected by a spiky case.

New ground

If a plant's seeds all dropped to the ground and grew there, they would soon choke each other. Seeds have the best chance of growing into new plants if they are scattered before they take root. The wind, animals and water all help to scatter seeds.

▲ Sycamore seeds (at the top) are spread by the wind. They have wings to help them fly further from the parent tree.

▲ Burdock seeds have small hooks which catch in an animal's fur.

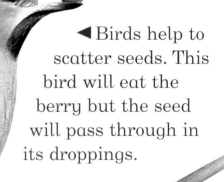

◄Birds help to scatter seeds. This bird will eat the berry but the seed will pass through in its droppings.

Some seeds are light and feathery and can be blown far by the wind. Animals scatter fruit seeds in their droppings. The seeds of plants that grow in or near water can float away to new ground.

▶ These coconuts floated across the sea and were washed up on the beach. They are now beginning to sprout.

◀ A bean seed begins to grow. First the root appears, then the shoot.

These are young beech seedlings.

Seedlings

Not all seeds grow into new plants straight away. Before it can grow, a seed needs soil, water and the right temperature. In countries where there are cold winters, seeds may wait until spring. In the desert, seeds wait several years for rain.

When a seed does begin to grow, it first puts down a root. Next a shoot pushes up into the air. As soon as the leaves open, the plant starts to make its own food (see page 8).

▼ The Kalahari Desert has very little rain. When it does rain, seeds quickly grow into plants and produce flowers and seeds.

World of flowers

There are about 250 000 different kinds of flowering plants and they grow in most parts of the world – on mountains, in deserts, in forests and in fields.

Only the icy Arctic and Antarctic are without flowers. We use flowering plants for food, clothes and medicines. Wheat, maize and rice are flowering plants, as well as cotton and tea.

◀ Bright red poppies grow in fields and on roadsides. Do not pick them – leave them to make seeds for the next year.

Glossary

Anther The tips of the stamens where pollen is produced.

Carbon dioxide A gas which is carbon and oxygen combined together. It is one of the gases found in air.

Carpel The female part of a flowering plant. Inside the carpel is one or more ovules. These are female seeds.

Chlorophyll The substance that makes plants green. It absorbs some of the energy of sunlight, especially in the leaves, which the plant uses to make food from carbon dioxide and water.

Fertilized A seed is fertilized when a female ovule joins with a male pollen cell from another flower of the same kind. Only fertilized seeds can grow into new plants.

Ovule The female seed or egg. It has to join with a male pollen cell from the same kind of flower to become fertilized and grow into a new plant.

Oxygen A gas which plants and animals need to breathe to stay alive. It is one of the gases found in air. Oxygen is produced by plants during photosynthesis.

Photosynthesis The name for the way plants make their own food using carbon dioxide and water plus the energy of sunlight.

Pollen Tiny grains produced in the anthers of flowers. A pollen grain contains two male pollen cells that must each join with a female seed to produce a new plant.

Spore Ferns, mosses and other kinds of non-flowering plants grow from spores. Spores are single cells which produce the male and female cells that are needed to make new plants.

Stamen The male part of a flowering plant. It is a stalk with an anther at the end. Pollen is produced in the anther.

Veins Thin tubes which carry liquid in a plant.

Key facts

Tallest tree Australian eucalyptus trees grow up to 132 metres high – nearly half as high as the Eiffel Tower in Paris and higher than St Paul's Cathedral in London.

Smallest flower Brazilian duckweed grows in water. The whole plant is no more than 0.6 mm wide and the flowers are even smaller.

Longest leaves True palm trees have no branches. Instead they have long leaves. The longest are those of the raffia palm, which grow up to 20 metres long – as long as two buses end to end.

Largest fruit The jackfruit is the largest fruit in the world. It grows in southern Asia. Each huge fruit can weigh up to 30 kilograms, which is about as heavy as an eight- or nine-year-old child.

Fastest growing plant Bamboo is a kind of grass. It can grow up to a metre a day. In just two days it would be taller than most adults.

Oldest tree Some bristlecone pines have been growing for more than 4000 years. They were seedlings when the pyramids of Egypt were built. They grow in California in the United States, but they are not flowering plants.

Most seeds A single orchid can produce a million seeds. The seeds are as small as pollen grains and blow a long way away in the wind.

Meat-eating plants Sundews, Venus fly-traps and pitcher plants are just some of the plants that trap insects. The insect's body slowly breaks down to give the plant extra minerals. The plant cannot get these minerals from the poor soil in which it grows.

Tallest cactus The giant saguaro cactus grows up to 18 metres high – as tall as a six-storey building.

Longest roots The African wild fig has roots which can grow up to 100 metres long – as long as a football pitch.

Index